Busines

Introduction to GNVQ: Advanced

GNVQ

Contents

Introduction

Welcome to the Advanced GNVQ in Business. We hope you will find this a stimulating and rewarding study programme. By following the course you will develop a range of knowledge, skills and understanding needed for working in business. You will also gain a clear insight into the whole professional business sector – how it is organised, and the sorts of jobs people do within it. This, we hope, will help you make important decisions about your own career.

You may already be quite familiar with GNVQs – perhaps you have completed a GNVQ at Foundation or Intermediate Level; you may have read or been told all about them. On the other hand as they are relatively new qualifications you may be unfamiliar with them. Either way, this induction booklet is designed to give you all the information you need in order to start your studies in a confident mood.

As you work through this induction booklet you will find out:
• what GNVQs are and how they are structured
• how you can use different strategies for learning
• how you will be assessed for your GNVQ
• how the Longman Study Units will help you with both learning and assessment
• how to develop your study skills.

You will notice that some terms or words in the booklet appear in bold type. You will find these terms explained in the Glossary at the end of the booklet.

1 What is a GNVQ?

GNVQs are qualifications that are being introduced throughout the United Kingdom. Their aim is to encourage people — especially young people — to learn about the skills and knowledge needed to work in particular areas of work. They are recognised, by employers and academic bodies, as the main national qualification for vocational education.

GNVQs cover a broad programme of study which will help you to prepare for the next stage in your career — whether you opt for further study, training or employment.

What does GNVQ stand for?

GNVQs have several important features which are described by the words which go to make up their full name.

General
GNVQs are general – they cover the broad range of skills, knowledge and understanding needed by those wishing to work in a particular vocational area such as business. They also cover wider skills, such as working with numbers, communication skills and using information technology effectively.

National
GNVQs are qualifications recognised throughout the UK. They are also identical throughout the country – someone in Cumbria studying for a GNVQ will work to the same standards as someone studying on the Isle of Wight.

Vocational
'Vocational' means linked to a job, occupation or career – in your case, business. GNVQs help you to investigate the kinds of tasks, roles and jobs of people working in this occupational area.

Qualification
When you have completed all the work on your GNVQ programme you will receive a qualification which is recognised throughout the country.

How do GNVQs relate to other qualifications?

There are three levels of GNVQs. Each level is roughly equivalent to other academic qualifications you may be more familiar with:

GNVQ level at:	*Is equivalent to:*
• Foundation level	four GCSEs at Grades D to G
• Intermediate level	four GCSEs at Grade C or above
• Advanced level	two A levels.

While most academic qualifications cover only one specific topic (e.g. A Level Biology, GCSE Communication Studies), GNVQs cover a broader selection of subjects. This is because they reflect the broad base of knowledge and skills needed to work in a particular occupational area.

Figure 1 shows how GNVQs fit into an overall national framework of qualifications.

Fig. 1 Three pathways in a national framework of qualifications

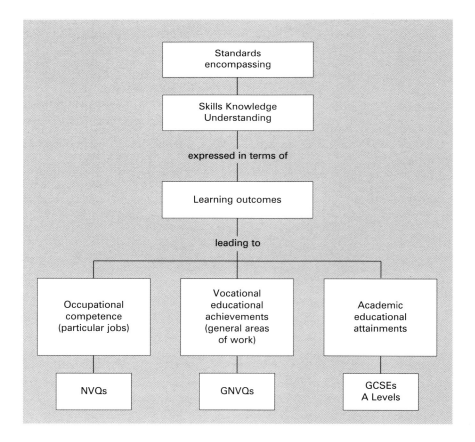

As you see, each route offers the chance for you to gain qualifications, which could be:

- occupational – NVQs (National Vocational Qualifications); these are similar to GNVQs, but are based more closely on work roles; they are intended mainly for people actually in work
- vocational – GNVQs at a higher level or in other occupational areas
- academic – GCSEs or A levels.

Because GNVQs are general and broad based, they open doors to a range of different career possibilities and other qualifications. After your GNVQ you can choose:

- an academic route – to move to further or higher education
- an occupational route – to start a career in the business professions
- a vocational route – to undergo further training in specific areas such as accountancy, banking or marketing.

Figure 2 illustrates some of the possible routes you can consider as you begin your Advanced GNVQ.

Fig. 2 Possible routes following completion of an Advanced GNVQ

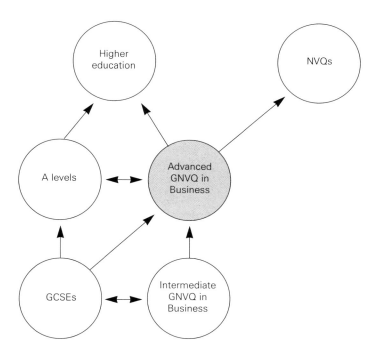

Activity

This activity will help you think about what routes you might consider. You may find it useful to carry out the activity with other students on your programme.

1 First make a list of jobs in the business professions that interest you, e.g. accounting technician, insurance clerk, export clerk, bank cashier, accountant, teacher, bank manager, retail manager, marketing manager, solicitor.
   What qualifications are needed for each job? Write the qualifications against the job titles you have listed. You may need the help of your teacher/tutor or a careers adviser to complete this task.

2 Bearing this in mind, which of the routes in the diagram do you intend to follow? Describe the qualifications you already have and which ones you might aim for in the future.

You may not have made any firm decisions about your future at this stage. However, it is useful to have at least some idea of what goals you are aiming towards.

The case studies on the next page describe how students can use GNVQs to develop their careers.

Awarding Bodies

Every GNVQ is given to successful students by an Awarding Body. Like A level examination boards they have a wide range of roles. For example, they:
- issue sets of **standards** which describe the skills and knowledge you need for a GNVQ
- specify the **optional units**
- organise tests which you will look at later in this booklet
- supply some of the documents you will use during your course
- award your final certificate when you have completed your GNVQ.

There are currently three Awarding Bodies for GNVQs. They are:
- City and Guilds of London Institute
- BTEC (Business and Technical Education Council)
- RSA (Royal Society of Arts) Examination Board.

They are all approved by the National Council for Vocational Qualifications (**NCVQ**), the organisation which monitors the whole system of vocational qualifications.

Activity

Find out which of the organisations listed above is your Awarding Body. Make sure that you have a copy of the booklet issued by your Awarding Body that contains the standards – you will need to refer to it constantly.

Shaheen wanted to have a career in either accountancy or European business. She passed five GCSEs in grades A-C in English Language, Modular Science, Art, and History. She knew that to gain entry on to degree programmes in either of her chosen areas, she needed to obtain good A Level results or an appropriate GNVQ Advanced course with either Merit or Distinction.

Shaheen was advised to do an Advanced GNVQ in Business. At interview she was told that to gain entry on to a degree course, she would need GCSE Maths grade C or above, and was advised to take this qualification which went well together with the Application of Number skill that she would study during her GNVQ course. Shaheen enjoyed the course and got her GCSE Maths at the end of the first year. She chose optional and additional units which were relevant to both the accounting and European business (which included languages). During her course she had two work placements, one within the finance department of her local authority and one working within the export department of a large business. She particularly enjoyed working with figures, working on the computers and working with, and learning from, people in work placement. In the autumn of her second year, Shaheen decided on her career route and applied for a degree in Accounting and Management Control. She was accepted by three universities.

James completed his Intermediate GNVQ in July 1995. He got a Merit grade and was particularly interested in retail management. The Advanced GNVQ seemed an excellent way of gaining a qualification that was relevant and could be used directly in this specific area of business. He also decided to study A Level Economics – he had been awarded a B in his GCSE Economics while he was working on the Intermediate level.

After leaving school at the age of 16 with some qualifications, **Gemma** had spent several years working in administration for a number of firms. Her aim was to become a teacher or lecturer in Business Studies so although she had a wealth of experience, she needed formal qualifications.

She decided to take the plunge and do a full-time course to help her achieve her goal. She saw the GNVQ as a way of getting used to studying full time again and also as a useful route to getting on to a teaching degree course at university in a couple of years' time.

2 How are GNVQs structured?

Every GNVQ is based on a set of standards developed by experts in the relevant vocational area. The standards are contained in a booklet published by the Awarding Body, mentioned in the last activity. The standards describe what you actually have to do in order to gain the qualification – i.e. your learning outcomes. The standards also describe the structure of the qualification. We will look at this next.

Units

Every GNVQ is made up of a number of **units**, each covering a specific topic. Every unit has a title and a number, e.g. Unit 5 — 'Production and Employment in the Economy'.

For an Advanced GNVQ, you need to complete fifteen units, as shown in Figure 3.

Fig. 3 The structure of an Advanced level GNVQ

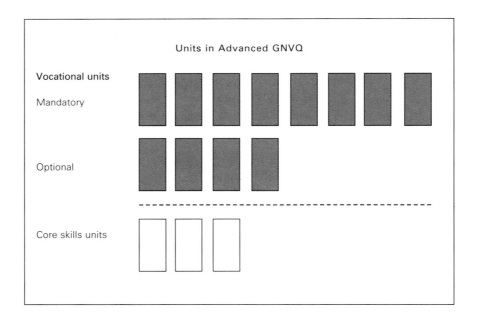

As you can see from Figure 3, there are different kinds of unit in one GNVQ. The main difference is between vocational and core skills units:

- **vocational units** – each unit covers a topic linked to the specific vocational area of business, e.g. for the GNVQ in Business topics include 'Human Resources' and 'Business Organizations and Systems'
- **core skills units** – each unit focuses on a skill useful to any vocational area, i.e. communication, application of number and information technology.

Every Advanced GNVQ student must do the eight mandatory vocational units, but you can choose which four optional units you study. The number of optional units you will have to choose from will depend on your Awarding Body. You will look at how to make your choice later.

Mandatory units

The eight mandatory units for the Advanced GNVQ are shown in Figure 4 below.

Unit 1	*Business in the economy*	This unit looks at the environment in which businesses operate and considers how governments (both UK and worldwide) influence businesses. You will have the opportunity to develop your own understanding of some fundamental economics, how and why governments attempt to influence the economy and how different economic relationships are built as businesses strive to achieve their own objectives.
Unit 2	*Business organisations and systems*	In this unit you will look at the different types of business organisations, who owns them, the way they are structured, and what makes them tick. You will investigate the types of systems set up within businesses to deal with the large amounts of information that they receive on a daily basis. This includes communications systems and the impact on businesses of electronic technology and information-processing systems.
Unit 3	*Marketing*	This unit looks at how important marketing techniques have become to the future success of business organisations, particularly in developing new products and modifying products. You will look at and evaluate marketing communications for different target audiences, and see how customer service is often crucial as part of the selling process.
Unit 4	*Human resources*	The success of any business is due, to a large extent, to its employees and therefore to a good human resource management function. You will look at job roles, changing working conditions and recruitment and selection. You will have the chance to practise job application skills, letter writing and the production of a *curriculum vitae*.

Unit 5	*Production and employment in the economy*	Businesses constantly seek to add value through increased productivity and new production methods, including new technology and working methods. The employment market is also changing fast, led by changing business needs. In this unit you will examine these effects on the employment market in the UK, compare the performance of the UK economy with major competitors in other parts of the world, and look at how the government seeks to affect and improve this performance.
Unit 6	*Financial transactions, costing and pricing*	This unit explains the importance of financial information to the financial transactions involved in business and looks at the costs of goods and services and the concept of added value from a financial point of view and how it is distributed. Businesses have systems to record financial transactions and you will look at the types of financial documents used within the system and have the opportunity to complete examples. By knowing the different compnents of the costs involved in producing their product, a business can calculate the breakeven point and make pricing decisions.
Unit 7	*Financial forecasting and monitoring*	In this unit you will look the finance needed to set up and run a business, and find out the usual sources of finance for different business organisations. You will look at the use of cash flow forecasts for budgeting, supporting business plans and forecasting. The unit introduces the formats used to show financial information in a business, and the use of financial ratios to interpret and monitor trends and situations of the business's performance that might need management attention.
Unit 8	*Business planning*	In this unit you consider all the aspects of setting up a small business and the production of a business plan. You will have the opportunity to identify a potential business opportunity and gather the information you need to make a detailed plan with appropriate resources and timescales taken into account. This unit will also help you to investigate and plan for employment or self-employment.

Fig. 4 The eight mandatory units for the Advanced GNVQ

Optional units

The four optional units you choose help you develop your skills in particular areas of interest by covering them in more detail. Examples of optional units are:

- creative marketing communications
- product development and realisation
- living and working in Europe
- behaviour at work
- foreign language: listening
- foreign language: speaking

- business and the law
- financial services.

The optional units available to you will depend on your school or college and on your Awarding Body.

Activity

Find out what optional units are offered by your school or college and make a note of them. Decide which of them you are most interested in studying and write down a brief description of each one. Your description should be similar to our description of the mandatory units in Figure 4.

Elements

Each unit is broken down into several **elements**. Each element covers one aspect of the unit topic.

Activity

In Figure 5 you can see the overall unit title for Unit 1. There are three elements in this unit. Look them up in your GNVQ Standards booklet and check the titles of the three elements.

Fig. 5 The elements in Unit 1

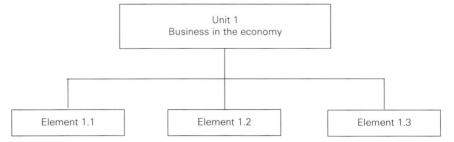

Each element clearly states the skills, knowledge and understanding that you need to gain credit for that part of the unit. It does this through:
- performance criteria
- range
- evidence indicators.

Performance criteria

Performance criteria (PCs) describe what you have to do in order to demonstrate your knowledge, skills and understanding for each element, i.e. the main learning outcomes. There are usually between three and six performance criteria in each element.

Activity

Look at your own set of standards. Find the performance criteria for Element 1.2.

What will you have to do to show that you can analyse the operation of markets and their effects on businesses and communities?

According to the performance criteria, you will have to:
• explain types of markets
• compare competition within markets
• analyse behaviour of businesses in different markets
• evaluate the social costs of market operations
• evaluate the social benefits of market operations.

Range

Activity

What types of markets would you have to explain? Look again at the standards for Element 1.2. Where does it give this information?

You will find this information in the range for the element. Here are listed the different types of market you need to know about, i.e:
• competitive
• non-competitive
• monopoly
• oligopoly.

The range goes on to list the competition within markets that you need to compare:
• for customers and sales
• for market share
• for product superiority
• for price
• between businesses to shift demand curves
• effect on consumers.

You will also find a list of factors of behaviour of businesses in different markets, to analyse in terms of:
• competitive price strategies
• price makers, price takers
• non-pricing strategies.

There is also a list of factors to use to evaluate social costs in terms of:
• effects on the environment
• effects on health
• effects on employment.

Finally, there is a list of factors to use to evaluate social benefits in terms of:
• effects on employment, investment, training.

As you can see, the range gives you vital information about the amount and type of knowledge you need for each element. The range helps you interpret the PCs. So, for the first PC in Element 1.2 – 'Explain types of markets' – the range tells you exactly which types of markets you need to know about.

For every unit and element you study you need to examine carefully the performance criteria and interpret them in the context of the range.

Evidence indicators

We have said several times that you need to demonstrate your knowledge, skills and understanding. But how do you do this? What evidence can you supply?

Activity

Look again at Element 1.2 in your GNVQ booklet. At the bottom of the page is a paragraph or two headed 'evidence indicators'. Read this through to find out about how you can prove your competence – the sorts of evidence you can supply. What does it suggest?

This paragraph states that you will need to do a report which will give a clear explanation of two markets in terms of numbers of suppliers in the markets; size of suppliers; and strength of demand in the markets. It should also compare two businesses in one market, showing shifts in demand curves, and explain why these shifts have occurred.

Your assignment must include a description of how the competition affects consumers' choice and the quality of products; pricing and non-pricing strategies to improve market position; and the costs and benefits to the wider community.

These evidence indicators are very useful. They tell you what sorts of activities or assignments you can do to demonstrate your knowledge and skills.

Look at some of the evidence indicators for other elements in Advanced Units 1 to 8. What kinds of things do they suggest you can do? Give an example of at least three different sorts of evidence.

You will have noticed a number of important forms of evidence:
- discussion – e.g. on why governments intervene in markets for Element 1.3
- report – e.g. one which identifies and explains types of employment, looking particularly at national and regional trends and their implications for Element 5.2
- case study – e.g. producing a capital budget, trading forecast and cash flow forecast for a twelve-month period for a small business for Element 7.2
- set of completed documents – e.g. for Element 6.2
- a draft business plan – for Element 8.1
- a presentation – e.g. about proposals for the development of one product, based on an analysis of market research information for element 3.2.

We will look in more detail at how you how you present evidence later in the booklet in the section on 'How you are assessed'.

The structure of a GNVQ unit is summarised in Figure 6.

Fig. 6 The structure of a GNVQ unit

Key:
PC = Performance Criteria

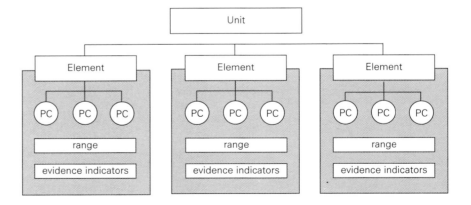

Core skills units

For an Advanced GNVQ you have to complete three core skills units at Level 3 or above. You can do core skills units at five levels altogether. Unlike vocational units, core skills units do not focus on aspects of business. Instead they are about skills that are essential for any area of work.

There are three additional core skills units:

- Personal skills
  – Working with others
- Personal skills
  – Improving your own performance
- Problem solving

You *can* gain credit for these but you don't *need* to complete them for an Advanced GNVQ.

The three core skills units you have to complete are:

- Communication (C)
- Application of numbers (AN)
- Information technology (IT).

If you are particularly good at one of the core skills areas, for example, computers (information technology) or communication, you can go on to take core skills units at a higher level once you have achieved the Level 3 core skills units. Taking higher levels will demonstrate to future employers just how good your skills are in certain areas.

Core skills units are made up of the same kind of sections as the vocational units. Each unit is broken down into elements, performance criteria and range. Figure 7 shows three examples of core skills elements.

Communication Element 3.2	Produce written material on a range of matters.	This is about writing memos, notes, letters and reports on routine things (as well as less common occurrences) using correct grammar and punctuation and appropriate emphasis.
Information Technology Element 3.3	Present information.	This is about deciding on the most appropriate way to convey written and graphic information clearly, and covers letters, diagrams, reports.
Application of Number Element 3.3	Interpret and present data.	This is about understanding, describing and using numerical information, including graphs, symbols, diagrams and three-dimensional objects as well as the concept of probability.

Fig. 7

Core skills and the vocational units

Core skills are practical skills which you develop and apply in all your GNVQ work, including your work on the vocational units. In fact the best way to show that you actually possess the core skills is through the work you do on the vocational units. The activity below will help you appreciate this connection.

Activity

In your GNVQ booklet, look at the standards for Element 7.4 – 'Identify and explain data to monitor a business'. The evidence indicator for this element says that you must describe the key components of information used for monitoring a business, explain who would want to use the information and why, and

why comparisons and variances can be useful when monitoring a business's performance. When you do this assignment you will have a good opportunity to apply and demonstrate your core skills. In particular, you could use the following skills:

- Communication, Element 3.2 – 'Produce written information'; and Element 3.4 – 'Read and respond to written material'
- Information technology (by producing your work using IT), Element 3.1 – 'Prepare information'; Element 3.2 – 'Process information; and Element 3.3 – 'Present information'
- Application of number, Element 3.2 – 'Tackle problems'; Element 3.3 – 'Interpret and present data'.

How do you think you could show these core skills as you prepare your evidence for this element?

If you use the *Longman Study Units* you will have plenty of chances to develop and use core skills.

If your evidence is in written form, e.g. your answer has taken the form of a report, you are bound to use communication skills. If you use a word-processor and perhaps spreadsheets, graphs and charts to illustrate how a business has performed, you are using and showing information technology skills. This element gives you the opportunity to provide evidence for numerical skills. Here is how one student approached the task.

Leslie decided to investigate different profitability, solvency and performance ratios to demonstrate how a business had been performing. To do this, he would need to have two sets of information so that he could make a comparison. In this case he had figures on a business for 1993 and for 1994. He did the research and prepared percentages which showed whether the business had made more or less profit than the previous year and whether the business was more or less efficient. He then looked at some other information on the business and calculated some more figures that highlighted where the managers of the business could make improvements. Leslie checked through his work thoroughly and made some alterations to his calculations before he finally presented his work in printed format for evidence. This meant that he had provided evidence for application of number skills.

Additional studies

As part of your course or programme, you may be doing some additional studies. This will depend on your school or college and on your Awarding Body, but they could include:

- GCSEs
- A Levels
- GNVQ additional vocational units
- GNVQ additional core skills units.

If you are interested in finding out more about the last two items on the list you should ask your tutor or supervisor.

3 The Longman Study Units

The *Longman Study Units* in this series have been specially prepared to encourage you to participate actively in your learning. If your school or college has decided to use the whole range of *Study Units*, you will probably use them in conjunction with classwork and other independent work. Your teacher or lecturer will guide you about when and how to use the *Study Units*.

The structure of the Study Units

The *Study Units* are based on the GNVQ Units at each level.
• Each *Study Unit* covers one GNVQ unit.
• Each section of the *Study Unit* covers the work of an element.

The *Study Units* have been designed to cover all the performance criteria and the range of a unit. As you work through each *Study Unit* you will gather evidence to gain credit for that unit.

The *Study Units* have particular features which are especially designed to help you both learn and gather evidence for your GNVQ award.

Activities An important feature of the Study Units is the regular **activities**. These are self-contained learning tasks which will help you develop your knowledge, skills and understanding of health and care. Activities can take many forms. Here are just a few examples:
• questions that ask you to think about issues or explore your own experiences
• role plays that give you the opportunity to dramatise and explore situations or feelings
• quizzes that help you check your knowledge
• group activities, e.g. brainstorms, discussions, debates, role plays
• case studies or scenarios that ask you to decide what you would do in a particular situation.

After each activity you will find some 'feedback'. This offers the author's suggestions, ideas or responses to the issues raised in the activity. Sometimes, where there are definite right or wrong answers, the feedback is located at the end of the *Study Unit*.

Figure 8 shows an example of an activity taken from Study Unit 8 - 'Business planning'. It encourages you to think about different types of mission statements, and the objectives that different organisations might have.

Fig. 8 An example of an Activity from Study Unit 8

Activity

Read the two mission statements, one for a profit-making business and the other for a school, and compare them in terms of:

- differences and similarities
- clarity
- are they realistic and achievable
- are they challlenging
- are they measurable (or supported by objectives that are measurable)
- are they prioritised so that there is no doubt about which objectives are most important?

Assignments

The *Study Units* also contain larger learning tasks called **assignments**. These are more open-ended and usually involve research into a particular topic.

An important aim of the assignments is to help you gather evidence to present towards your GNVQ. You will see that the assignments often link very closely with the evidence indicators for each element.

Figure 9 shows an example of an assignment from Study Unit 1 – *'Business in the Economy'*

3.1, 3.2, 3.3, 3.4 C ⓒ **Assignment**
3.1, 3.3, AN

For this assignment you will need to carry out research to compare the decision-making process concerning competition supply and demand of British Rail (before privatisation) to run the line servicing the Channel Tunnel and a major supermarket chain expanding its market share by developing new sites.

1 **Find out the size and number of suppliers and the strength of demand in these two markets. Illustrate your findings.**

2 **How do businesses influence demand? What pricing and non-pricing strategies do they use to improve their market position?**

3 **Describe how competitive positioning and techniques affect consumer choice and the quality of products produced.**

4 **a Discuss the social costs and/or benefits to the wider community of the business decision of the supermarket chain to open a new store in an area.**

   b What would the costs and benefits be if the chain closed a similar store in a different area to that community?

Present your report in a 5–10 minute presentation. Look at such factors as:

• the number of jobs created or lost
• traffic or other environmental considerations
• convenience of supply
• any other social costs or benefits you have found to be important.

Fig. 9 An example of an assignment from Study Unit 1

Core skills

The *Study Units* have been designed to help you combine working on the vocational units with developing your core skills. You will have plenty of opportunities to apply core skills as you work through particular assignments and activities.

Core skills checklist

Table 1 shows how all the core skills are covered by the *Longman Study Units*. When you have completed each *Study Unit*, you should check that you have covered the core skills suggested for that unit. You may like to photocopy the checklist so that you can use the final column to record which core skills you have covered. Write down a reference to say which assignment or activity covered the core skills.

At the end of each Study Unit in the review activity is a summary of all the core skills elements you should have covered in the unit. There is also a reminder to make a record of which core skills you have covered.

Table 1: How core skills are covered by Longman Study Units

Communication

Element	Title	Longman study unit	Check
3.1	Take part in discussions	Unit 3: Marketing (3.1, 3.2) Unit 1: Business in the economy (1.3) Unit 8: Business planning (8.3)	
3.2	Produce written material	Units 1-8	
3.3	Use images	Unit 6: Financial transactions, costing and pricing Unit 3: Marketing Unit 5: Production and employment in the economy	
3.4	Read and respond to written material and images on a range of matters	Unit 3: Marketing Unit 5: Production and employment in the economy Unit 1: (1.1, 1.2) Unit 7: Financial forecasting and monitoring	

Information technology

Element	Title	Longman study unit	Check
3.1	Prepare information	Unit 8: Business planning (8.2) Unit 7: Financial forecasting and monitoring Unit 2: Business organisations and systems Unit 4: Human resources (4.3)	
3.2	Process information	Unit 8: Business planning (8.2) Unit 7: Financial forecasting and monitoring	
3.3	Present information	Unit 8: Business planning (8.2) Unit 7: Financial forecasting and monitoring Unit 2: Business organisations and systems	
3.4	Evaluate the use of information technology	Unit 7: Financial forecasting and monitoring (7.4) Unit 8: Business planning (8.2) Unit 2: Business organisations and systems	

Application of number

Element	Title	Longman study unit	Check
3.1	Collect and record data	Unit 8: Business planning (8.1, 8.2) Unit 6: Financial transactions, costing and pricing (6.1) Unit 5: Production and employment in the economy (5.3) Unit 3: Marketing (3.2, 3.3)	
3.2	Tackle problems	Unit 6: Financial transactions, costing and pricing Unit 7: Financial forecasting and monitoring Unit 8: Business planning (8.1, 8.2) Unit 3: Marketing (3.2)	
3.3	Interpret and present data	Unit 6: Financial transactions, costing and pricing Unit 7: Financial forecasting and monitoring Unit 8: Business planning (8.1, 8.2) Unit 3: Marketing (3.2, 3.3) Unit 5: Production and employment in the economy Unit 1: Business in the economy	

4
How will you be assessed?

Assessment is the way your achievements are measured and judged. It is also the way you gain feedback to find out how you are doing. You may be familiar with assessment which involves tests or examinations. However, you may also have experienced more continuous forms of assessment, e.g. through coursework for GCSEs, which gives an assessor a clearer picture of what you can do over a period of time.

The assessment process

GNVQs incorporate both forms of assessment, with a strong emphasis on coursework. Assessment for GNVQ involves:
- gathering and presenting evidence from projects and **assignments** – for each element you produce work which fully covers the PCs and range
- taking tests – eight of the mandatory units have a one-hour test set by the Awarding Body.

Because of this emphasis on gathering evidence, you take a very active part in all your learning and assessment. You can make choices about the sorts of assignments you undertake and the kinds of evidence you collect.

You can take as long as you like to gather evidence and pass the tests, although in practice you will probably follow a GNVQ programme in a school or college lasting for two years.

Stages in the assessment process

There are several stages in the assessment process. These are illustrated in Figure 10.

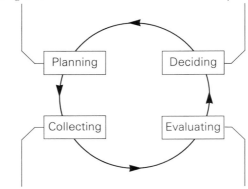

Fig. 10 Stages in the assessment process

4 Deciding
Your teacher or lecturer looks over your evidence, makes recommendations, gives you feedback and then records your achievements. If he or she decides that you need to do more work or present different evidence, you will go back to Stage 1 for that part of your work.

1 Planning
You will begin the process by drawing up an Action Plan for collecting evidence.

2 Collecting
As you work through your GNVQ programme you collect evidence of your achievements on the units. We will look at this in more detail in the section called 'Gathering evidence'.

3 Evaluating
You (and your teacher) will need to check that the evidence you have gathered actually does match the performance criteria and range statements to the appropriate standard.

As you see, assessment is an ongoing process. As you go through your course, you continue to plan, collect evidence, receive feedback and decide what to do next. You will also note that for coursework you are assessed by your own teacher or lecturer.

Activity

Look at the performance criteria for Element 2.2, 'Investigate administration systems'. What kind of evidence do you think you might produce for the PCs in this element?

Begin to draw up a plan, including any ideas for finding information, how long it might take you, etc.

You could decide to produce evidence such as:
- a report on an administration system of an actual business organisation
- a poster or diagram outlining the legal and statutory requirements
- a questionnaire analysis showing how well the individuals in the chosen organisation think the system works
- a presentation to your group on your findings.

You could then carry out research:
- in the library
- by writing to national organisations (such as the Health and Safety Executive) and investigating local contacts (such as a trade union representative)
- by getting permission to make appointments with key staff members within your chosen organisation, to ask questions
- getting the questionnaires completed and analysed.

Finally, you could allow yourself a week to gather all your information together and two weeks to word process your report, prepare your poster or diagram and prepare for your presentation.

You will need to go through this process every time you collect evidence.

Tests   Tests are set by the Awarding Body. They assess your knowledge and understanding of the vocational units, e.g. through multiple-choice questions. Units are tested and assessed separately so you can gain credit for one unit at a time. Your assessor will enter you for the test when you both feel you are ready. Your test will be marked by a computer. The results will be published and returned within 30 days.

Activity

You will find it helpful to learn what sort of tests your Awarding Body sets. Ask your teacher or lecturer to tell you what the tests involve and to show you specimen papers and answer sheets, so that you know what to expect when you come to take the tests.

Collecting evidence

Throughout your work on GNVQs you will collect evidence to demonstrate that you have met the requirements set out in the standards. This evidence can take many forms: reports, posters, graphs and charts, art or design work, cassettes, videos, photo albums, diaries, and so on.

You will also collect records of grades, tests, notes from your assessor and perhaps from a supervisor where you do work experience.

You may be able to use evidence from outside your GNVQ course – from school, from a part-time job or from your general life experience. We will go into this in more detail later.

All this evidence needs to be gathered together into a **portfolio of evidence**. Since you will be collecting a considerable amount of evidence, you will need to think about the best way to store it all. You may, for example, need:

- a lever arch file for ordinary written work and records
- a large box for storing videos or three-dimensional objects which you create
- an artist's portfolio for work which is larger than A4.

Organising evidence

Your portfolio will need to be well-organised so anyone looking through it can easily find what they want. It should also be easy to see how the evidence relates to the PCs and range of particular units and elements.

Here are a few tips about organising your evidence.

- Organise your evidence unit by unit, and element by element. This keeps all the different material separate.
- Set up a system right at the start of your programme.
- Keep your storage and filing system up to date.
- Use dividers in files and other labels to identify evidence.
- Include a list of contents and index at the front of the file.
- Keep your evidence secure – the evidence you collect is valuable!

Activity

Give some thought to how and where you will store your evidence. Make a note of your decisions. Work through the points above to outline how you will organise your evidence. You may have boxes or files which you could use, or you may be able to borrow them from friends or family.

Once you have got well into your programme you may find you have to re-organise your evidence – for example, if you find your files bursting at the seams.

Keeping records

Both you and your assessor need to keep careful records of your work on the GNVQ. You will find that you need to use a number of forms to record all the essential information. These forms will vary depending on whether they come from the Awarding Body or have been designed by your school or college. They may have different names and appearance, but here are some of the common forms you may use.

- *Portfolio log sheet or Cumulative Assessment Record* – This is where you keep an up-to-date record of your progress. You record the work you have done, the date you completed each piece of work, the evidence you collected, where this evidence is stored, and so on.
- *Action Plan and review* – Here you record your plans for each piece of work. You also record the actual outcomes of each activity and suggest any further action to be taken.
- *Grading record sheet* – This is a record of the **grading themes** you have covered, i.e. planning, using information, etc. We will look at grading later.
- *Unit completion record* – You will need to record the units you have completed and the tests you have passed. This form is your claim for the GNVQ.

Activity

Find out what forms are used in your school or college for recording GNVQ work. If possible, gather samples of each one. You may find it hard to understand what they are for until you have had them explained to you or have actually used them, but you will soon become accustomed to them.

Who assesses you?

You are the first person responsible for your assessment. It is your task to create and collect appropriate evidence and to organise it in your portfolio. In fact, in assessing you, your assessor will consider how much responsibility and initiative you have shown in your work. However, there will be people available to help you at each stage of the process.

Assessor

Your teacher or lecturer is known as your assessor. Your assessor will:
- help you plan your work
- discuss opportunities and activities for assessment
- guide you in selecting evidence to present.

Your assessor will look at all the evidence you collect and will check your work against the GNVQ standards. He/she will then offer feedback and suggestions as to any improvements you could make.

Your assessor then decides whether your evidence is up to the standards required by the Awarding Body and will record your achievements.

Internal Verifier

The Internal Verifier helps and supports your assessor in thinking of opportunities for you to gather evidence for your portfolio. He or she may be an assessor for the same or a similar course as yours, who ensures that the same standards are being met across the course in a school or college.

External Verifier

The External Verifier comes from the Awarding Body to make sure that your assessment is fair. He or she comes into schools and colleges to look through samples of work and ensures that the same standards are being met throughout the country.

Action Planning

You will be aware by now that planning is an important part of success in GNVQs. It is also a skill you need for any job or course of study, as well as in everyday life.

Activity

Assume you are planning a backpacking holiday abroad with some friends. This is not unlike a GNVQ assignment in that it includes a number of different things to think about.

Break this assignment down into smaller tasks. When you have done this, think about the order in which you will need to do each task. Write down your list of tasks, in order. Opposite each task, say what skills you think you will use to carry it out.

Table 2 shows our ideas of the tasks (in order) and the skills involved in planning a backpacking holiday.

Table 2: Tasks involved in planning a backpacking holiday

Tasks	Skills
apply for a passport	prioritising, filling in forms
find out about the different holidays available	seeking information, carrying out research
discuss with your friends and choose where you want to go	communicating, negotiating, organising information
find out whether you need a visa	finding information
buy some maps	social and number skills
work out an itinerary	planning
find out whether you need any vaccinations	finding information
buy a backpack	identifying necessary items
find out what the local travel situation is like in different countries	research
arrange insurance cover	communication skills
buy new clothes for the holiday	identifying necessary items
get local currency	identifying necessary items and numeracy skills
arranging transport to the airport	seeking information

Action Plans can take many forms depending on the size of the task involved:
• It may be a simple list of tasks written on a sheet of paper.
• You may use a diary, calendar or wall planner to outline your learning and assessment activities over several months.

This list can also form the basis for an Action Plan since it lists the major tasks you have to complete to have a successful holiday and the skills you use to complete the tasks. The same applies to your GNVQ studies: Action Plans will help you to decide on, plan, manage and monitor your own learning.

The first sort of plan, listed in the margin, would be suitable for one part of an assignment for one element, whereas the second Action Plan could cover your plans for several GNVQ units.

At the beginning of your programme you will mainly work on substantial, long-term Action Plans. As you progress into the individual units and elements, you will draw up more detailed Action Plans, including specific dates for completing tasks. For example, if you are using the *Longman Study Units*, you should draw up an Action Plan for every assignment you undertake.

You will have to review your Action Plans often and use them as the basis for organising your work, to assess what progress you are making and to decide what you still have to achieve.

Figure 11 is one possible format for an Action Plan. Alternatively, you may prefer to design your own personal form and have it photocopied a number of times.

Fig. 11 Example form for an Action Plan

ACTION PLAN				
Name _____				
Unit/Element _____				
Performance Criteria covered		Range covered		
Aim of project/work		Core skills I could cover		
What do I have to do?	What order will I do it in?	When will it be done by?	Who will do it ?	Tick when done
Deadline for completion				
Resources needed				
Changes I made to my action plan				
Signed student				
Signed tutor				

Activity

Look at the sample assignment in Figure 9, taken from Study Unit 1, 'Business in the Economy'. Imagine you have to start this assignment. You want to complete it within two weeks from today. Use a blank form like the one above to write an Action Plan for this assignment. Include your overall aims for the assignment and then list the individual tasks you will need to complete, with the target dates. Refer to the standards for Element 1.2 in your GNVQ booklet to find out more details about the range for this element.

You may have found this quite a taxing activity, especially if you have not attempted an Action Plan for some time. Action planning can be a difficult exercise — you have to think really hard about what you are going to do.

When you look closely at an assignment like this one, it is surprising how many different tasks have to be planned. Here are some you may have included in your Action Plan.

As a final point, remember that good Action Plans will help you get a good grade, so it is worth investing time in learning how to draw them up.

- Decide what information you need to find out about the two markets you are investigating, such as the approximate size of the market in value terms, the number of suppliers and their market share, and where you will look to find out the information.
- Look at the range to find out about the pricing and non-pricing strategies you will need to include, and find out more about them.
- Think about the steps you need to take to find out how competitive positioning and techniques affect customer choice and quality of product produced. Are you going to carry out some observational research in a supermarket, or look at similar transport examples to the Channel Tunnel situation, for example?
- Identify what research you need to carry out in order to look at the social costs and benefits to the community of a new supermarket store.
- Use resources such as the library, the business advisor at your local bank, newspapers, maps of your area.
- Decide on a format - how will you structure your report? How will you prepare the diagrams and graphs illustrating your findings?
- Arrange to book time on a computer (make sure you allow enough time).
- Create your final report, following your outline format and including the illustrations you have prepared.
- Remember to include all your information sources.
- Allow sufficient time to check your work.

Learning log/diary

Many people who plan well also keep a learning log or diary. This is a place where you can:
- note points you want to talk over with your tutor
- remind yourself to do things
- write down any questions or problems that occur to you.

You can use an ordinary diary or a notebook to make these notes. You can make notes anywhere and at any time. A small, pocket notebook is especially useful for jotting down your thoughts while you are on work placements.

Grading

If you complete all the work on the vocational and core skills units, pass the tests and successfully present your portfolio of evidence, you automatically receive a Pass grade for your GNVQ. However, you can gain higher grades: either a Merit or a Distinction. These grades are awarded to candidates who show particular skills in areas of:

- *Planning*
1 drawing up plans of action
2 monitoring courses of action
- *Information seeking and information handling*
3 identifying information needs
4 identifying and using sources to obtain information
- *Evaluation*
5 evaluating outcomes and justifying approaches
- *Quality of outcomes*
6 synthesis
7 command of language (concepts, forms of expression and presentation).

The GNVQ grading criteria focus on the ways in which you tackle activities. They are very useful for future employment. They provide a measure of how you go about planning, carrying out and evaluating your work. They also focus on how successfully you have brought together these aspects to produce your work in your folders.

In order to gain a Merit grade you have to show that you can:

Merit
- independently prepare action plans for a series of separate tasks and put them in order of priority
- monitor your work and recognise when you need to change your action plan. Your tutor can help you
- decide, without help, what information you will need
- find and collect the information that you need
- make sure that your work meets the requirements of the tasks you have to do
- justify what you do
- identify and consider alternatives
- bring together relevant knowledge, skills and understanding in the work that you have done
- communicate confidently in the concepts, forms of expression and presentation of 'business' at Advanced level.

Distinction
If you are hoping to gain a Distinction you will have to show that you can deal with complex activities involving more than one task at a time. You will have to:

The main differences between a merit and a distinction are:

1 how well you deal with complex tasks
2 how well you work independently.

- independently prepare action plans for the activities and put them in order of priority within the time allowed
- independently monitor your work and recognise when you need to change your action plans
- decide, without help, what information you will need
- independently find and collect the information that you need, using a range of sources and justify their selection
- make sure that your work meets the requirements of the tasks you have to do, stating the advantages and disadvantages of the methods you have used, identifying alternatives and improvements
- bring together relevant knowledge, skills and understanding in response to complex activities
- communicate fluently in the concepts, forms of expression and presentation of 'business' at Advanced level.

'Discrete' tasks are straightforward and contained in a single stage, while 'complex' tasks have several parts and include a number of different skills. It is the difference between, say, switching on the kettle (a discrete task requiring only one skill) and making a cup of tea (a more complex task in several stages requiring several skills).

As your assessor works through your portfolio of evidence he/she will record evidence which meets the criteria for a merit or a distinction. These records become part of the evidence you submit for final assessment and verification.

At least one third of your work on the mandatory and optional units will have to show evidence of your skills in planning and handling information.

At the moment, you may lack confidence in your skills in these areas, but you will be developing them as you work through your course. If you have done the Intermediate GNVQ, you will be familiar with these approaches to work and will be able to build on your existing experience.

Since your grade is determined by one third of your work on the mandatory and optional units, much of the evidence might be collected in the later parts of your work. However, you should try to develop and use these skills right from the start of your Advanced GNVQ work.

5 How will you learn?

GNVQs may appeal to you because they relate to life outside school or college. GNVQs also have a unique — and stimulating — approach to what you learn and how you learn it.

Your GNVQ programme is intended to give you knowledge in a broad occupational area, i.e. business. The best way to do this is to learn as much as possible about this area of work. You will do this partly through your own reading, investigation and research. At the same time, work experience will give you real first-hand experience of what is involved in business.

Your learning on the Advanced GNVQ programme will be varied – and above all, active. A wide range of activities and assignments should contribute to a rich experience of learning and discovery.

Your learning may involve the following activities:
- work experience, which could include visits, a placement or 'shadowing' someone in their job
- taking part in seminars by people who work in business
- group work and group discussions
- watching videos or TV programmes about business issues
- surveys and interviews with clients, people who work in organisations, people who own their own businesses and the general public
- research or investigation into a particular aspect of business
- drawing up case studies
- writing reports and summaries
- creating other materials – posters, leaflets, audio tapes, videos
- carrying out role plays – to help you to feel what it might be like in certain situations
- visits – to libraries, businesses and statutory bodies.

While you are doing all these things, you are gathering evidence that will help you gain a nationally recognised qualification, as well as preparing yourself for a job or career.

Although you are ultimately responsible for your learning, this does not mean that you will be left to do everything yourself. Your teacher or lecturer will teach some classes, run workshops, lead discussion groups or organise visits or practical sessions. In any case, he or she will be available to help you with anything you are uncertain of. *The Longman Study Units* will also help you to learn and to gather evidence in an organised way.

6 Study skills

You have already gained many skills, both inside and outside school. If you have studied GCSEs or Intermediate GNVQs you will be familiar with planning your work, reading and investigation, using computers and some aspects of design and technology. The Advanced GNVQ will help you to build on the skills and knowledge you have already gained and apply them to practical, work-related situations.

Research

One area which often gives students cause for concern is carrying out research. Many of the projects ask you to carry out research into some aspect of business. Without realising it, we are all doing research almost constantly — we need to acquire information, seek the answers to our questions and organise the information we have gained into some sensible order. You are probably an experienced researcher already!

So, for example, if you are asked to carry out some research on factors affecting individuals' choice of a particular product, you simply need to work independently to find out more about it. You may need to organise interviews or talk with people, visit a library, listen to radio or watch TV programmes. When carrying out research, often the methods you use are almost as important as the information you come up with, so don't forget to consider how you will carry out your investigations. You will also need to know the difference between primary and secondary sources and their relative importance. Secondary research is using other people's work; so, for example, consulting books in the library is secondary research, but interviewing people is primary research. The *Longman Study Unit* on Marketing will help you practise your research methods.

As long as you organise your work and go about it with a clear plan in mind you should not encounter any difficulties. Your action planning skills will be very valuable here.

Activity

One part of an assignment completed for Unit 8 asked students (who were working in small groups) to produce a marketing plan for a small business's product. Here is how one group of students approached this assignment.

The purpose of the activity

By producing a marketing plan for our business plan, we hope to be able to support our original idea with clear indications of how, where and to whom the product will be marketed and sold.

What is needed?

In our group, in order of priority, we need to:
1 Read through the range to see what factors to consider.
2 Produce a detailed breakdown of the demand for the product.
3 Negotiate who does what and when.
4 Look at the marketing mix – pricing, packaging, distributing, promotion, and discuss suitable ideas for the product. Decide how to present evidence – in this case a presentation.
5 Research the costs of an appropriate marketing campaign – contact advertising agencies, local radio, bus company, newspapers, TV, printers for costs and times of printing.
6 Include a realistic timing schedule and flow chart.
7 Identify the budget needed for our proposed campaign. Decide what after-sales support is needed for this type of product and company.
9 Identify plans for reviewing and monitoring progress.Draw up an outline marketing plan, with visual displays to show the information we have gathered and illustrate our marketing communications plans.
10 Allow time to check our work.
11 Practise presentation.

Word processing and use of other software packages will take place throughout the assessment.

Areas of difficulty

1 being able to apply the theory to our business plan
2 obtaining costs of advertising
3 completing the reviewing and monitoring section
4 being able to identify an appropriate calendar for advertising.

Standards

We will know we have achieved the required standard when we have checked, ticked off, and completed the evidence required to meet the performance criteria and range and have used information technology to complete the assignment.

You can see that a research task like this, which seems enormous at first, can be broken down into smaller tasks which are easier to complete. Use this method for any research project — or whenever you need resources of any kind. Your teacher or lecturer is likely to be the first person you ask about how to track down a book, a video or a piece of equipment. But there are other people you can ask, such as the librarian and people from whom you can acquire personal information directly.

You may have to be quite persistent at times in order to find out what you need to know, but most people are only too happy to help. When you are asking people for help, always explain that you are following a GNVQ programme. Explain the purpose of your research. Reassure them that you will give credit for any information they provide which you include in your final assignment evidence and that you will respect any confidentiality requirements.

Making presentations

Some of the projects and assignments you do will involve finding information, which you are then asked to present to other people. Often a presentation will simply be to other members of your study group.

Many people find this a stressful and difficult task. It is almost impossible to remove tension from this situation, but there are lots of practical steps you can take to ensure that presentations go well.

- Organise your information well in advance:
  - make clear notes, e.g. use small cards for the key points you want to make
  - get any handouts, charts or other papers in order
  - if you are using aids, like overhead projector slides, tapes or videos, have them all ready and to hand.
- Practise in advance by making your presentation to a supportive audience, e.g. to yourself in the mirror, to a friend or relative, or a collection of stuffed toys!
- Time yourself carefully, to see that you have enough time for what you want to say.
- Where possible, use audio-visual aids to present information.

For example, you could use a flipchart or overhead projector to:
  – present the key points of particular topics
  – show a diagram, graph or chart
  – give an overview of information.
• If you do use audio visual aids, follow a few simple rules:
  – think about how much information you will present in this way; don't try to do too much
  – check your equipment is working before the presentation
  – don't stand in front of the screen, flipchart or board.

One way of reducing the pressure of a presentation is to give it jointly with another student or a group of students. This halves the pressure at a stroke, making you feel much less vulnerable.

Respecting confidentiality

As you go about your investigations, you should appreciate that some information may be confidential – especially information about individuals. Always check on this and reassure people that you will respect their privacy.

Financial information about individuals or businesses is particularly private. You will almost certainly not be allowed to see salary or financial records unless you have the agreement of everyone concerned, above all that of the individual and managing director. You may be allowed to cite confidential information as long as you don't use any names.

Always explain what you want from people and what you plan to do with the information, especially if you are hoping to video or record them. Ask if they mind their names or their experiences being included in your portfolio of evidence. Many people will not mind at all, but others may be sensitive and ask you to change their names or leave out certain details which could identify them.

References

It is clear that you will be relying on many other sources of information to build up the evidence for your GNVQ. It is essential to acknowledge sources of information which you use, whether the source is, for example, a person, a book or journal, a television programme or newspaper clipping.

People   Always acknowledge any help you have received from anyone. You can simply list the names of people who have helped with your work with a note such as: 'I would like to thank the following people for their help'. The only exception to this rule is when confidentiality is an issue. You may be able to substitute another name; this can be as simple as 'Business X' or 'B'. If an official from any organisation has helped you, note the name of the organisation, and the person's job title, e.g. 'I would like to thank Margaret Stewart, Production Director at Morehams Agriculture Ltd for her help'.

Written materials   Whenever you use a book, article, pamphlet or magazine you should always mention it in your work. Your reference may appear either where the quote actually appears, or in a separate references section at the end of your report, or both. Your reference must include the following information:
- author's name
- title of book

or
- title of article and name of magazine or journal
- date of publication
- publisher.

Here are two examples, one from a book, one from a newspaper:

Charles Handy, *Inside Organisations, 21 ideas for Managers.* (1990) BBC Books

'Trouble Brewing for Chancellor'. *Daily Telegraph*, 17 May 1994.

Other sources of information

You may also wish to refer to television or radio programmes, even videos. Give as much information as you can, including:
- the name of the programme or video
- when it was broadcast and by whom
- name of film production companies such as Universal Studios or MGM.

For example:

Panorama, 18 June 1995, BBC.

7 Building on earlier experience

When you begin your Advanced GNVQ programme, you will bring to it a lot of knowledge and experience. You have had many years at school, you may have completed the Intermediate GNVQ, you may have had a job or done some voluntary work, perhaps in some area of selling or administration or maybe in a completely different field of work. Perhaps you have been involved in a scheme like the Young Enterprise Scheme. In any case, you have already gained skills and understanding which will be of help with your GNVQ.

Accreditation of prior learning

You may be able to use this knowledge as evidence of your skills in certain areas – provided that you have some proof, such as written work, letters, photos, certificates or other records. These can be included in your portfolio of evidence.

If you do collect evidence from earlier experience, it will be assessed against the GNVQ standards, like all the evidence you collect. You will probably have to answer questions to prove that the evidence is genuinely yours. This is known as **Accreditation of Prior Learning**, or **APL**. You will need specialist help in accumulating evidence of prior learning – there is a special assessor for this process.

Activity

Think of all the things you do now or have done in the past which could be relevant to your Advanced GNVQ programme. List these activities or experiences. What evidence do they provide of your skills and knowledge?

Relevant experiences could include:
• projects undertaken on previous work experience
• charity fundraising
• a job (part-time or full-time) dealing with the public or handling money
• taking part in a Young Enterprise Scheme

- doing the family food shopping
- a Duke of Edinburgh Award
- voluntary work
- doing a newspaper round
- helping the family business.

You may have certificates or badges, or references from people you have worked with. These could all contribute to your assessment.

You will need to discuss with your assessor any evidence of past experience you present. He or she will give you guidance about how relevant or useful it is.

Summary

You should now feel well prepared to begin your Advanced GNVQ programme. You know about most of the important features of GNVQs and how they differ from other qualifications. You should be familiar with the structure of GNVQs – including units, elements, performance criteria and range. You should also be clear about the difference between vocational units and core skills units and the way they are combined to form one qualification.

You have seen how GNVQs are assessed and how you play a very active role in assessment. You have begun thinking about building up your portfolio of evidence.

You have thought about active learning and seen that you will be responsible for many aspects of your GNVQ programme. Finally, you have seen that you already have skills and knowledge which you may be able to count towards your GNVQ.

We hope that you will go ahead with confidence and use your GNVQ to take a positive step towards your chosen career.

Review activity

This induction unit contains a lot of information. Much of it will be new to you and you will need some time to absorb it. There may be aspects of GNVQs that you are still unsure about. Scan quickly back through this booklet and make a note of any points you don't fully understand. Use the following headings as a checklist for your points.

Points to follow up

1 **What is a GNVQ?**
2 **How are GNVQs structured?**
3 **The Longman Study Units**
4 **How will you be assessed?**
5 **How will you learn?**
6 **Study skills**
7 **Building on earlier experience.**

There are many ways you can resolve these queries:

- in discussion with your teacher or lecturer
- by talking to more experienced GNVQ students
- by re-reading the relevant parts of this booklet
- by reading other documentation, e.g. from the school, college or Awarding Body.

Many of these points will fall into place as you get underway with your work on the GNVQ units. We wish you every success!